UK PREMIERE
PRODUCED BY
THE CORONET THEA

YOUTH WITHOUT GOD

A PLAY BY
CHRISTOPHER HAMPTON

BASED ON THE NOVEL BY
ÖDÖN VON HORVÁTH

DIRECTED BY
STEPHANIE MOHR

CAST

Heinrich Reiss
Owen Alun

Robert Ziegler
Raymond Anum

Arno Feuerbach
Brandon Ashford

Julius Caesar / The Headmaster / The Priest / The Prosecutor / An Inspector
David Beames

Herr Neumann, a baker The Sergeant / The Defense Counsel / The Trauners' Butler / A Policeman
Christopher Bowen

Otto Neumann
Malcolm Cumming

Franz Bauer
Finnian Garbutt

Eva
Anna Munden

Dieter Trauner
Nicholas Nunn

Nelly, a prostitute / Frau Trauner / Frau Ziegler
Clara Onyemere

The Teacher
Alex Waldmann

CREATIVE TEAM

Writer
Christopher Hampton

Director
Stephanie Mohr

Set and Costume Designer
Justin Nardella

Lighting Designer
Joshua Carr

Sound Designer
Mike Winship

Casting Director
Serena Hill

Assistant Director
Harriet Taylor

PRODUCTION TEAM

Head of Production
Andy McDonald

Company Stage Manger
Emma Smith

Deputy Stage Manager
Isobel Hodgkiss

Assistant Stage Manager
Camilla Direk

Chief Electrician
Alex Ramsden

Costume Supervisor
Megan Sayers

Production Photography
Tristram Kenton

Graphic Design
Will Mower

Youth Without God was first performed at Theatre in der Josefstadt on 26 Nov 2009.

The UK Premiere was at The Coronet Theatre on 23 Sep 2019.

With thanks to:
Mel Kenyon and all at Casarotto Ramsay & Associates

Supported by the
Austrian Cultural Forum London

CAST

Owen Alun *Heinrich Reiss*

After almost 10 years on *Rownd a Rownd*, a soap opera for S4C, Owen Alun attended Rose Bruford College and graduated last year with a First-Class honours degree. His theatre credits include: *Twrw Dan a Dicw* (Fran Wen), *The Girl with the Incredibly Long Hair* (We Made This). For television: *Almost Never* (Saltbeef Productions). As a voice over artist: *Dragons Riders of Berk* (Lefel Dau).

Raymond Anum *Robert Ziegler*

Raymond Anum trained at RADA. He is making his professional stage debut in *Youth Without God*. His credits while training include: *Othello*, *All My Sons*, *The Last Days of Judas Iscariot*, and *Much Ado About Nothing*.

Brandon Ashford
Arno Feuerbach

Brandon Ashford has recently graduated from Guildhall School of Music and Drama, and he is making his off-West End debut in *Youth Without God*. His drama credits whilst training include Iago in *Othello*, Pylades in *Orestes*, Lola in *Mercury Fur*, David in *After The Dance*, Terry in *Merrily We Roll Along* and Bill in *Kiss Me Kate*. At the Edinburgh Fringe Festival (2018) Brandon played Pork Chop in *Born On A Monday*, which he also co-wrote and co-directed. Brandon is also the winner of The Josephine Hart Poetry Competition 2018.

David Beames
Julius Caesar / The Headmaster / The Priest / The Prosecutor / An Inspector

During his long acting career David Beames has regularly performed at the Royal Court, National Theatre, the Globe, RSC and West End. Recent theatre credits include: *Happy Days* (Young Vic) and *The Neither* (Royal Court and West End). Film & TV credits include: *Holby City, Justifying War – Scenes from the Hutton Inquiry, Pie In The Sky, Casualty, Miss Marple, Destiny, Submariners* (BBC); to name a few.

Christopher Bowen
Herr Neumann, a baker / The Sergeant / The Defense Counsel / The Trauners' Butler / A Policeman

Theatre credits: *Mrs Warren's Profession* (Everyman), *Macbeth* (Southwark), *The Country* (Belgrade), *Hamlet* (Young Vic/Tokyo), *Franziska* (Gate), *Antony and Cleopatra/The Shrew* (Haymarket), *Private Lives* (Palace Watford), *She Stoops to Conquer* (Salisbury), *Much Ado About Nothing, Cyrano de Bergerac* (RSC European Tour and Broadway) *Macbeth, Peer Gynt, Softcops, Moliere, The Body,* (All RSC). Television: *Outlander, Endeavour, Ransom, Trust, Maigret Sets a Trap, Homefront, Parade's End, Lewis, Jane Eyre, Poirot, Soldier Soldier, The Shell-Seekers, Dr Who, Tanamera.* Film: *On Chesil Beach, Hitler: Rise of Evil, Tomorrow Never Dies, Richard III, Cold Comfort Farm.*

Malcolm Cumming
Otto Neumann

Malcolm Cumming trained at the Royal Conservatoire of Scotland. He spent the last year working as the Robertson Trust Graduate Actor with the Citizens Theatre. Productions included: *Cyrano de Bergerac, The Dark Carnival, A Christmas Carol.*

Other theatre includes: *Lord of the Flies* (Matthew Bourne's New Adventures), *Sunshine on Leith*, *Spring Awakening* (Captivate, Ed-Fringe). Cumming received best actor award at the Scottish Short Film Festival for *Spaceship* and played the lead in the feature *Anna and the Apocalypse* for MGM. Malcolm is also a writer, producing work for the BBC.

Finnian Garbutt *Franz Bauer*

Finnian Garbutt trained at the Royal Welsh College of Music and Drama; he received the Emma Style Award and FinTru Theatre Bursary whilst studying. He is making his professional stage debut in *Youth Without God*. Credits whilst training include: *All My Sons* (dir. Dave Bond), *RAGE* (Simon Stephens UK Premiere dir. Elle While), *Machinal* (dir. Sean Linnen), *Turbines* (dir. Emily Ling Williams), *The Sicilian Courtesan* (dir. Laurence Boswell). Radio credits: *Last Orders* (dir. Philip Crawford), *Bog Child* (BBC Radio 4 Book At Bedtime). Television credits: *Rockumentary* (dir. Owen Franklin)

Anna Munden *Eva*

Anna Munden started her career with Pipeline Theatre Company, touring three shows nationally from 2013-2015. These included: *Transports*, *Streaming*, and *Spilikin* (which was shortlisted for the Carol Tambour Best of Fringe award). In the summer of 2016 she played Abigail in Cube Theatre's production of *The Crucible*. She completed a BA in Acting at Bristol Old Vic Theatre School in 2018. Since graduating Munden played East in *You Promised* (Theatre 503) and lead roles in short films *Keeping Up The Act* and *Shoal*.

Nicholas Nunn *Dieter Trauner*

Theatre credits include: *Hotel Paradiso* (Drama Centre); *Twelfth Night* (Drama Centre); *The Rivals* (Drama Centre); and *Buffer* (Thrive Theatre). Television and film credits include: *World on Fire*, *The Victim*, *London Kills*, *Clique*, *Misbehaviour*.

Clara Onyemere *Nelly, a prostitute / Frau Trauner / Frau Ziegler*

Theatre credits include: *Risk Assessment* (RADA Festival); *Mary Wollstonecraft* (Unitarian Church); *Chicken* (Hackney Empire); *Unstated* (Red Room); *Richard III* (Southwark Playhouse); *Six Acts of Love* (Tron Theatre); *Masks* (Oval House); *Uncle Vanya* (Babel Theatre); *Witch* (Watermill Theatre); *Orestes* (Shared Experience); *Snow Queen* (Manchester Library); *Blood Wedding*, *Fuente Ovejuna* (National Theatre). Clara is a co-founder of Immediate Theatre. TV and Film credits includes: *Liar*, *Breeders*, *MotherFatherSon*, *Our Girl*, *Wolfblood*, *Come Home*, *Lucky Man*, *Cuffs*, *iboy*, and *Molly*.

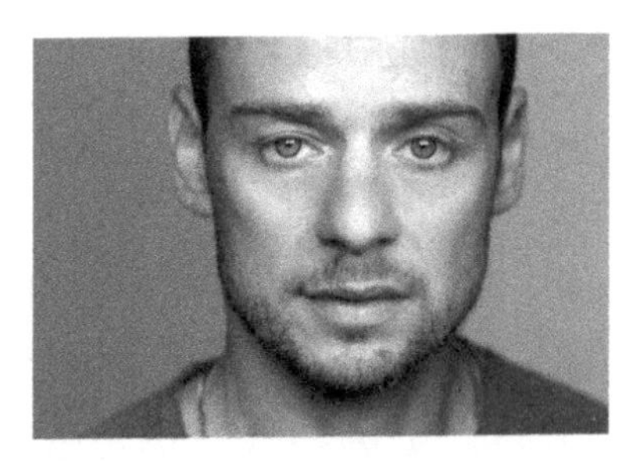

Alex Waldmann *The Teacher*

Alex Waldmann trained at LAMDA. Theatre credits include: *Julius Caesar*, *All's Well That Ends Well*, *As You Like It*, *Hamlet*, *King John*, *Richard III* (RSC); *All My Sons*, *Wars of the Roses* (Rose Theatre); *In The Night Time* (Gate Theatre); *Widowers Houses* (Orange Tree); *Jonah and Otto* (Park Theatre); *King John*, *Knight of the Burning Pestle*, *Duchess of Malfi* (Globe Theatre); *Holy Rosenbergs* (National Theatre); *Speechless* (Shared Experience); *Rope* (Almeida Theatre); *Hamlet*, *Twelfth Night* (Donmar West End); *Troilus & Cressida* (Cheek by Jowl). Television includes: *Strike Back*, *Humans*, *Duchess of Malfi*, *The Night Watch*, *Psychoville*, *First Light*.

CREATIVE TEAM

Christopher Hampton *Writer*

Christopher Hampton wrote his first play, *When Did You Last See My Mother?* at the age of eighteen. Since then, his plays have included *The Philanthropist, Savages, Tales From Hollywood, Les Liaisons Dangereuses, White Chameleon, The Talking Cure, Appomattox* and *All About Eve*. He has written the libretti for three Philip Glass operas and co-written three musicals including *Sunset Boulevard*. He has translated plays by Ibsen, Molière, von Horváth, Chekhov, Yasmina Reza (including *Art* and *God of Carnage*), Daniel Kehlmann (*The Mentor, Christmas Eve*) and Florian Zeller (*The Father, The Mother, The Truth, The Lie The Height of the Storm and The Son*). His plays, musicals and translations have garnered four Tony Awards, three Olivier Awards, four Evening Standard Awards and the New York Theatre Critics' Circle Award. Hampton's many screenplays include: *Dangerous Liaisons, Total Eclipse, The Quiet American, Atonement, Chéri* and *A Dangerous Method*. He both wrote and directed *Carrington, The Secret Agent* and *Imagining Argentina*. His television work includes adaptations of *The History Man, Hotel du Lac* and *The Thirteenth Tale*. Prizes for his film and television work include an Oscar, two BAFTAs, a Writer's Guild of America Award, the Prix Italia and a Special Jury Award at the Cannes Film Festival.

Stephanie Mohr *Director*

Stephanie Mohr was born in Genoa and grew up in Paris and Vienna. She trained as an Assistant Director at Austria's National Theatre, the Burgtheater, and has since been directing in Vienna (Theater in der Josefstadt, Volkstheater, Burgtheater, Schauspielhaus), Frankfurt, Mannheim, Klagenfurt, Nuremberg, Salzburg, Kiel, Linz, Lucerne, Bochum, Duisburg (Ruhr Triennale), Munich (Gärtnerplatz Theater, Kammerspiele) and Aix-en-Provence.

Awards include: Kainz Medal for *Knives in Hens*, Karl-Skraup Prize for *Attempts On Her Life*, Nestroy Special Prize for *Die Weberischen*, Nestroy Prize as Best Director for *Woyzeck & The Tiger Lillies*.

Most recent work includes *King Lear* in Klagenfurt, Max Frisch's *Andorra* in Linz, *Faith and Homeland* by Karl Schönherr, Felix Mitterer's *Jägerstätter, The Boxer* and *In der Löwengrube*, as well as *Seven Seconds of Eternity* by Peter Turrini, all at the Theater in der Josefstadt, Vienna. *Youth Without God* is Stephanie's UK debut.

Justin Nardella *Set and Costume Designer*

A graduate of the National Institute of Dramatic Arts, Sydney, Justin Nardella has worked internationally in his field. Theatre credits: *Eugene Onegin* (Buxton International Festival), *La Traviata* (Theatre Des Champs-Elysées, co-scenographer), *Songs For Nobodies* (West End), *Le Grand Mort* (Trafalgar Studios), *The Hunting of the Snark* (West End, UK Tour, Hong Kong, Australia), *The Life* (Southwark Playhouse), *Depths of Dead Love* (The Coronet Theatre), *Legends!* (Australian Tour), *Mr Incredible* and *Where Do Little Birds Go?* (Lonsight Theatre), *Hansel and Gretel* (Opera in Space), *Tender Napalm* (Brisbane Festival), *Orfeo* (Brandenburg Orchestra). He is the international associate on *Priscilla Queen of the Desert* the Musical. Projections: *Gianni Schicci* and *La Bohéme* for iSING Festivals Asia. Film: *Andy X* (Dir. Jim Sharman), *Spoilers* (Dir. Brendon McDonall) The *Scare's Could Be Bad* music video (Dir. Tom Noakes). Awards: BMW Young Artists award and William Fletcher Grant.

Joshua Carr *Lighting Designer*

Recent credits include: *Hamlet* (Leeds Playhouse); *True West* (Vaudeville Theatre); *Dealing With Clair* (Orange Tree Theatre); *Sweet Charity* (Nottingham Playhouse); *Hangmen* (Atlantic Theatre Company, New York); *A Christmas Carol* (Hull Truck); *Tiger Bay* (Wales Millennium Centre & Cape Town Opera); *Terror* (Lyric Hammersmith); *Romeo and Juliet* (West Yorkshire Playhouse); *Everybody's Talking About Jamie* (Sheffield Theatres); *Henry V* (Regent's Park); *Hangmen* (Royal Court & West End); *Lunch and the Bow of Ulysses* (Trafalgar Studios); *Wonderman* (Gagglebabble, National Theatre of Wales & Wales Millennium Centre); *Raz* (West End); *Songs For The End Of The World* (Vault Festival, Battersea Arts Centre); *Dinner With Friends* (Park Theatre); *Albert Herring* (RCM); *The Dissidents* (Tricycle Theatre); *The Caucasian Chalk Circle*, *Britain's Best Recruiting Sergeant* (Unicorn Theatre); *The Wasp*, *In the Vale of Health* (Hampstead Theatre); *The Realness* (Big House Theatre Company); *Exit The King* (Theatre Royal Bath); *Yellow Face* (National Theatre, Park Theatre).

Mike Winship *Sound Designer*

Recent sound designs include: *#HonestAmy* (Pleasance, Edinburgh); *Sonny* (ArtsEd); *Anatomy of a Suicide* (Central School of Speech & Drama); *Anna X* (Vault Festival); *The Jumper Factory* (Young Vic); *The Winter's Tale* (National Theatre & Schools Tour); *The Mysteries* (Manchester Royal Exchange); *The Human Voice* (Gate);

Zoo (Theatre 503); *Shadows* (Eurydice Speaks) (Schaubühne, Berlin). As Associate Sound Designer: *Macbeth*; *Hedda Gabler* (National Theatre UK & Ireland Tours); *The Girl on the Train* (West End/UK & Ireland Tour); *The Hairy Ape* (Park Avenue Armory, New York). Other sound work includes: Sound design for Bastille's Doom Days Amazon Music album launch campaign; Binaural sound recordist for Opera North's Aeons sound walk, as part of the Great Exhibition of the North 2018; Assistant sound designer on Land Rover's binaural Discovery Adventures podcast.

Serena Hill *Casting Director*

Serena Hill recently returned from Australia where she worked as the Casting Director at the Sydney Theatre Company. Since returning she has worked as a freelance Casting Director and recently credits include: *Dealing with Clair* by Martin Crimp for the Orange Tree Theatre and English Touring Theatre, *The Glass Piano* by Alix Sobler and *Youth Without God* by Christopher Hampton at The Coronet Theatre, *Valued Friends* by Stephen Jeffreys at the Rose Kingston, *Macbeth* at the Chichester Festival Theatre and *Dirty Crust* by Clare Barron at the Yard Theatre. Prior to living in Australia, Serena was Head of Casting at the National Theatre.

Harriet Taylor *Assistant Director*

Harriet is a graduate of New York University's Tisch School of the Arts, where she studied musical theatre at the New Studio on Broadway. After working on Broadway at general management firm Richards/Climan, Inc. and off-Broadway as a performer and arts administrator at New York Classical Theatre, she moved to London and completed her MA in Text & Performance at The Royal Academy of Dramatic Art. Since graduating she has appeared in BEAM and NMDP showcases, directed new work at the Camden Fringe, The Cockpit Theatre, Bloomsbury Festival, The Old Red Lion, Theatre 503, and the Actor's Centre's John Thaw Initiative, and played Claire in *Ordinary Days* at Soho Upstairs. She has most recently undertaken an MFA in Creative Producing at the Royal Central School of Speech and Drama. Harriet now works as Assistant Producer at The Mono Box and produces a monthly #networkshop series with her theatre collective Nothing to Perform.

THE CORONET THEATRE

The Coronet Theatre is a risk-taking, international theatre in an iconic, Grade II listed building in London's Notting Hill. We produce an eclectic programme of theatre, dance, music, poetry and visual art in our intimate 195-seat theatre and 90-seat studio, The Print Room.

A fusion of multi-disciplinary, international work, we stage exciting, often undiscovered pieces, crossing borders and defying expectations. Supporting established artists and nurturing new talent, we provide a hub for artists and the local community.

The Coronet Theatre combines grand architecture with an intimate and warm setting, featuring candlelit hallways, antique décor, stage props and the most beautiful theatre bar in London.

Founder and Artistic Director Anda Winters' personal curation of both the programme and building creates memorable and often unexpected experiences from the moment you step inside, and offers an uniquely welcoming space for audiences and performers.

103 Notting Hill Gate
London W11 3LB

thecoronettheatre.com
020 3642 6606

We are a registered charity no. 1141921

SUPPORT US

The Coronet Theatre is a place like no other.

Our programme is a fusion of drama, music, poetry, dance and visual art from new and established artists alike.

Our productions give audiences the chance to see the best of international talent in our intimate setting.

Our building has a rich history and offers a unique experience to all those who visit.

But as a charity, we need your help.

Become a supporter and enjoy a closer relationship with The Coronet Theatre by joining our Patrons scheme, making a donation or becoming a corporate partner.

To find out more, get in touch with the Development Team on **020 8051 0466** or **giving@thecoronettheatre.com**

THANK YOU

We would like to thank our Patrons for their support of our work:

Cupola
Clive & Helena Butler, Deborah Curtis, Michael Fisher, Mimi Gilligan, Ian Hannam

Proscenium Arch
Peter Davies, Connie Freeman, Victoria Gray, Kathryn Ludlow, Whitney McVeigh, Jane Quinn, Julia Rochester, Antony Thomlinson, Patrick & Anna Thomson

Royal Box
Ryan Allen, Tony & Kate Best, Bruno & Christiane Boesch, Thomas & Maarit Glocer, Peter & Tanya Freeman, Ashish & Neha Goyal, Debbie Hannam, Georgia Oetker, Reid Perper & Maria Clara Tucci, Dag & Julie Skattum.

Outreach supporters
Douglas Clarisse, The John and Lorna Trust

And to all our Stage Door Members and other donors who would prefer to remain anonymous.

STAFF

Artistic Director & CEO
Anda Winters

Interim Executive Director
Nick Williams

Producer (maternity leave)
Ella Minton

Producer (maternity cover)
Hetty Shand

Associate Producer
Cathy Lewis

Programming Coordinator
Julia Gillespie

Poetry Coordinator
Marion Manning

Bookkeeper
Andrew Michel

Head of Production
Andy McDonald

Chief Electrician
Alex Ramsden

Master Carpenter
Rodger Pampilo

Head of Development
Jemma Tabraham

Development Manager
Ilaria Pizzichemi

Press Representative
Sharon Kean

Marketing & Digital Officer
Kasia Mroczkowska

Venue Marketing
The Cogency

Box Office Manager
Nicola Courtenay

Box Office Assistant
Joe Hodgson

Facilities and Operations Manager
Hannah Shirer

Premises Assistant
Ramirez Rolando

Duty Managers
Jamie Fletcher, Joshua Manning,
George Rennie, Julia Sztucka,

Front of House Staff
Victoria Bell,
Freddie Butler-De-Lacy,
Natalie Chan, James Cooper,
Matilde Correia, Manuel DeCara,
Tylor Deyn, Olita Garkalne,
Juliet Hague, Elliot Hall,
Richard Leeming, Ruby Lovett,
Sam Sheldon, Rose Whiffen

VOLUNTEERS

Jelena Bogunovic, Jayne Neville,
Fiona Sandilands, Jan Winter

TRUSTEES

Youth without God

Ödön von Horváth (1901–1938) was born in Fiume, which was then part of the Austro-Hungarian Empire, of an aristocratic Hungarian-speaking family. His plays include: *Italienische Nacht* (*Italian Night*) 1931, *Geschichten aus dem Wiener Wald* (*Tales from the Vienna Woods*) 1931, *Kasimir und Karoline* (*Casimir and Caroline*) 1932, *Figaro Lässt sich Schieden* (*Figaro Gets a Divorce*) 1937, and *Don Juan Kommt aus dem Krieg* (*Don Juan Comes Back from the War*) produced 1952. Von Horváth's plays were banned when the Nazis came to power, then neglected in Germany until the 1950s.

Christopher Hampton was born in the Azores in 1946. He wrote his first play, *When Did You Last See My Mother?*, at the age of eighteen. Since then, his plays have included *The Philanthropist*, *Savages*, *Tales from Hollywood*, *Les Liaisons Dangereuses*, *White Chameleon*, *The Talking Cure* and *Appomattox*. He has translated plays by Ibsen, Molière, von Horváth, Chekhov, Yasmina Reza, Florian Zeller and Daniel Kehlman. His television work includes adaptations of *The History Man* and *Hôtel du Lac*. His screenplays include *The Honorary Consul*, *The Good Father*, *Dangerous Liaisons*, *Mary Reilly*, *Total Eclipse*, *The Quiet American*, *Atonement*, *Cheri*, *A Dangerous Method*, *Carrington*, *The Secret Agent* and *Imagining Argentina*, the last three of which he also directed.

also by Christopher Hampton

CHRISTOPHER HAMPTON: PLAYS ONE
(*The Philanthropist*, *Total Eclipse*, *Savages*, *Treats*)
TALES FROM HOLLYWOOD
LES LIAISONS DANGEREUSES
WHITE CHAMELEON
THE TALKING CURE
APPOMATTOX
A GERMAN LIFE

screenplays

COLLECTED SCREENPLAYS
(*Dangerous Liaisons*, *Carrington*, *Mary Reilly*,
A Bright Shining Lie, *The Custom of the Country*)
TOTAL ECLIPSE
THE SECRET AGENT & NOSTROMO

translations

Ödön von Horváth's
TALES FROM THE VIENNA WOODS
DON JUAN COMES BACK FROM THE WAR
FAITH, HOPE AND CHARITY
JUDGMENT DAY

Yasmina Reza's
'ART'
THE UNEXPECTED MAN
CONVERSATIONS AFTER A BURIAL
LIFE X 3
THE GOD OF CARNAGE

Ibsen's
HEDDA GABLER
A DOLL'S HOUSE
THE WILD DUCK
AN ENEMY OF THE PEOPLE

Chekhov's
THE SEAGULL
UNCLE VANYA

Molière's
TARTUFFE
DON JUAN

Daniel Kehlman's
THE MENTOR
CHRISTMAS EVE

Florian Zeller's
THE MOTHER *and* THE FATHER
THE SON
THE TRUTH
THE LIE
THE HEIGHT OF THE STORM

CHRISTOPHER HAMPTON

Youth without God

based on the novel
Jugend ohne Gott
by
ÖDÖN VON HORVÁTH

FABER & FABER

This edition first published in 2019
by Faber and Faber Limited
74–77 Great Russell Street
London WC1B 3DA

Typeset by Country Setting, Kingsdown, Kent CT14 8ES
Printed in England by CPI Group (UK) Ltd, Croydon CRO 4Y

A CIP record for this book is available from the British Library

ISBN 978-0571-35822-9

2 4 6 8 10 9 7 5 3 1

For
MARIA TEUCHMANN
and
IAN HUISH
friends to Horváth

Foreword

Odon von Horváth's 1937 novel *Jugend ohne Gott* (*Youth without God*) was the indirect cause of his extravagantly bizarre death.

Essentially a man of the theatre, Horváth had no doubt grown dispirited at the fact that very few of the nine plays he had written since the advent of the Nazi government in 1933 had reached the stage; indeed, one of the best of them, *Glaube Liebe Hoffnung* (*Faith, Hope and Charity*), which was in rehearsal in Berlin when the new regime came to power, had been immediately suppressed, before it even had a chance to open. So it's no surprise that he eventually turned to writing novels (there was another, *Ein Kind Unserer Zeit* (*A Child of Our Time*) that came hard on the heels of the first). The instant enormous success of *Jugend ohne Gott* must have come as a particularly welcome surprise to a man in the throes of extricating himself from post-Anschluss Vienna (where he had moved, from Germany, in 1933); and his trip to Paris to meet Robert Siodmak (one of the many German film-makers on his way to Hollywood) to discuss making a film based on the book must have been undertaken with considerable relief and optimism.

Before setting out from Amsterdam, however, incurably superstitious, Horváth had consulted a clairvoyant; she became extremely excited and told him that waiting for him in Paris was the greatest adventure of his life. Apparently, the lunch with Siodmak went extremely well; afterwards, at Siodmak's enthusiastic insistence, Horváth went to a cinema on the Champs Elysées to see the latest sensation, *Snow White and the Seven Dwarfs.* As he walked back to his hotel, meditating perhaps on the future of the animated film, a thunderstorm broke out; Horváth chose to shelter beneath a chestnut tree in the Avenue Marigny, a branch of which fell on his head, killing him instantaneously. He was only thirty-six.

An especially unusual feature of this most unusual life story is that, almost alone among the major German-speaking writers, Horváth chose not to go into immediate exile when the Nazis came in. There's no clear indication of why he decided to stay: 'It's going to be a very interesting time,' he wrote to a friend. 'Soon, you'll see, there'll be subjects lying around in the street', and it's my theory that he couldn't tear himself away from the grotesque idiocies and brutal illogicalities of a moronic and truculent regime – we perhaps have an inkling of how that feels today. Still, staying to observe everything at first hand was not without its difficulties: readers of his biography in the seventies were dismayed to discover that he had joined (as presumably one had to, to be able to pursue his profession) the Reichsverband deutscher Schriftsteller, the Nazi writers' union.

His background was impeccably anti-Nazi: in the twenties, he'd been in court for brawling with fascists, at least two of his plays – *Sladek* and *Italienische Nacht* (*Italian Night*) – are straightforward attacks on the right, and his pre-Nazi plays all bear witness to the growing political dangers threatening Germany and Austria. No writer since Flaubert had such a feel for the ignorant clichés of the prejudiced and self-righteous: so the thirties under Hitler must have provided him with an irresistible blank canvas. But the Anschluss, the demented enthusiasm with which Hitler was welcomed in Vienna, must have been the last straw and he left for Amsterdam with his girlfriend (his wife, he always maintained, he had only married to supply with a Hungarian passport, so that she, in turn, could make her escape). In Amsterdam were the émigré publishers Allert de Lange; they published the novel in the autumn of 1937. In a draft of an introduction, later abandoned, Horváth wrote: 'Since this book is about ideals, it's bound to be widely banned. It's a book against the illiterates, that's to say the people who know very well how to read and write, but don't know what they're writing and don't understand what they're reading. I've written a book for the young because . . . out of the stupidities and crap of their predecessors, a new youth is emerging. My book is dedicated to them!' He was expelled from the Nazi writers' union for never paying his subscription.

Thomas Mann wrote to Carl Zuckmeyer to say he thought *Jugend ohne Gott* was the best novel of recent years – and he wrote to Horváth to ask how he had come by such a wealth of inside knowledge. It's not known what, if anything, Horváth said in reply, but he must have been gratified not only by this response but also by the enthusiastic praise of Hermann Hesse, Franz Werfel and Joseph Roth, who, in a review, called Horváth 'the most clear-sighted chronicler of his age'. A French critic, Jean-Claude François, said he was the black-box (flight recorder) of the Third Reich.

Horváth had wanted to come to Britain, but the Home Office, no more enlightened then than now, refused him a visa. So he was no doubt on his way to America, where, in fact, I imagined a life for him in my play *Tales from Hollywood*. I've always been moved by what he wrote to his best friend Franz Theodor Csokor a few weeks before his death: 'The main thing, my dear old friend, is work! And furthermore, work! And once again, work! Our life is work, without it there can be no life. It makes no difference whether it brings us triumph or even attracts attention – it makes not the slightest difference, as long as our work remains dedicated to truth and justice. As long as we stay afloat, we'll always have friends and we'll always have a home, because we carry it with us – our home is the imagination.'

It still seems to me an exemplary credo for a writer.

Christopher Hampton

A Note on the Language

In the original 1939 English translation (by R. Wills Thomas and curiously titled *The Age of the Fish*), Chapter One is called 'Niggers': this is also the last word of the novel. Elsewhere, Thomas has translated the same German word (*Neger*) as 'Negroes'. As the use of this word in its most offensive form is more or less the inciting event of the story, I have retained it as a term used by the Nazi characters. Elsewhere, at moments of officialese, I have also used the word 'Negroes'; but, in addition, when the central character, the Teacher, uses the same expression, I have translated it as 'Africans'.

Youth without God was first presented in the UK at the Coronet Theatre, London, on 23 September 2019. The cast, in alphabetical order, was as follows:

Heinrich Reiss Owen Alun
Robert Ziegler Raymond Anum
Arno Feuerbach Brandon Ashford
Julius Caesar / The Headmaster / The Priest / The Prosecutor / An Inspector David Beames
Herr Neumann / The Sergeant / The Defence Counsel / The Trauners' Butler / Policeman Christopher Bowen
Otto Neumann Malcolm Cumming
Franz Bauer Finnian Garbutt
Eva Anna Munden
Dieter Trauner Nicholas Nunn
Nelly / Frau Trauner / Frau Ziegler Clara Onyemere
The Teacher Alex Waldmann

Director Stephanie Mohr
Set and Costume Designer Justin Nardella
Lighting Designer Joshua Carr
Sound Designer Mike Winship
Casting Director Serena Hill
Assistant Director Harriet Taylor

The play was first performed at Theater in der Josefstadt, Vienna, on 26 November 2009.

Characters

The Teacher

His pupils

Franz Bauer

Arno Feuerbach

Otto Neumann

Heinrich Reiss

Dieter Trauner

Robert Ziegler

Nelly
a prostitute

Julius Caesar

The Headmaster

Herr Neumann
a baker

The Sergeant

The Priest

Eva

The Public Prosecutor

The President of the Juvenile Court

The Defence Counsel

The Prosecuting Counsel

Frau Neumann

Frau Ziegler

The Trauners' Butler

Lola
another prostitute

A Policeman

An Inspector

Frau Trauner

Other boys, a pianist, court officials,
reporters, policemen, a female prison warder, etc.

If an interval is required, it should be taken
after Scene Eleven

YOUTH WITHOUT GOD

ONE

A plainly furnished bed-sitting room at the top of a house in a small town in southern Germany. It's March 1935. On the table in the window are a vase of flowers and a pile of school exercise books. The occupant of the room, the Teacher, perches on one corner of the table, looking straight out at us. He's thirty-four, inconspicuous enough, but his mild manner conceals a sardonic intelligence and an underlying dismay at the foolish ways of an irrational world, a map of which is the only visible decoration in the room.

Teacher Hello. So, the world seems to be spiralling towards disaster again, doesn't it? Although what do I know, I'm a teacher. As a matter of fact, it's my birthday today. Hence the flowers. From my nice old landlady. And this – (*He picks up an envelope from the table.*) is a letter from my parents. My mother says: (*He opens the letter and reads.*) 'I wish you all the best, my dear child, on your birthday. May Almighty God grant you good health, good luck and happiness!' And my father says: 'My dear son, all best wishes on your birthday. And may God Almighty grant you good luck, happiness and the best of health!' Well, we can all use a bit of luck and my health is excellent, touch wood. But happiness? That's a bit ambitious, isn't it? I can't say I'm really happy. But then, who is? I have a friend who says happiness is a purely economic matter. But there must be more to it than that, wouldn't you think? Anyway, whatever happiness is, it keeps well away from me.

Stupid to think that way, really. After all, I have a secure job at the local high school, and these days that's not to be sneezed at. Lots of people would give their eye-teeth to be in my shoes. I teach history and geography to fifteen-year-old boys and it's straight sailing all the way to my pension.

He reaches for the first exercise book on the pile.

Today's topic was: 'Why do we need colonies?' Let's see what . . . (*He consults the front page of the exercise book.*) Franz Bauer has to say on the subject. Franz Bauer says, here we are, 'We need colonies to supply us with raw materials, because without raw materials our manufacturing sector would no longer be able to function at full capacity, which would lead to a catastrophic return to former levels of unemployment. The whole state would be affected, as the workers form a vital element of our nation.' He's just trotting out what he reads in the paper and hears every day on the radio. So, well done, Franz Bauer! Quite right! Top marks!

It'd be more than my job's worth, as an employee of the state, to raise any objection to these mindless refrains. But there was, I must say, one of these essays that had me reaching for my red pen. Where is it? (*He pulls an exercise book out of the pile.*) Here it is, yes, Neumann. Otto Neumann, father's a baker, who likes to dress up in one of those hideous uniforms on his day off. Anyway, this is Otto Neumann's contribution. (*He reads from the exercise book.*) 'All niggers are cowardly, cunning and lazy.' Idiot. Anyway, as I say, I was about to strike out this contemptible piece of nonsense and write 'untenable generalisation' in the margin, when my hand suddenly froze in mid-air. Hadn't I just heard something very similar broadcast over the radio? I had. So I put down my pen. Wouldn't do for a mere teacher to question an opinion this moron probably copied down direct from the radio. I don't say I like the way things are, but you know, what good can one man do?

TWO

The noisy racket of rowdy schoolboys precedes the lights going up on a scene of chaos. In an austere classroom in the high school, more than a dozen pupils are shouting, scrapping with each other, banging desks and throwing chalk. Our attention is particularly drawn to a downstage group, where four of the boys are physically attacking Arno Feuerbach, one of the smaller pupils, holding him down on the floor, under the fishy eye of Dieter Trauner, a tall, sinister-looking boy with a disturbingly intense manner. At a certain point, Trauner drops to one knee, opens Feuerbach's lunch-box, which is on the floor beside him, takes out a bread-roll, no doubt containing Feuerbach's lunch, brandishes the roll in front of the struggling boy, opens the window – through which, now the noise has somewhat subsided, comes the sound of heavy rain – and throws the roll out into the courtyard below. Laughter from Feuerbach's tormentors, who return to their task of kneeling on him, slapping his face, pulling his hair, etc. Trauner continues to watch, with obvious fascination. The noise level rises again.

The Teacher steps into the room and sizes up the situation instantly.

Teacher What's going on here? Stop this immediately!

The boys break off their attack reluctantly, clambering sheepishly to their feet, finally allowing Feuerbach to scramble up, plucking anxiously at his torn collar.

If you absolutely have to fight, be so good as to follow the elementary principles of single combat, not five against one, that's just cowardly.

The Teacher puts his briefcase on his table and unfastens the clasps.

What did he do to you, anyway?

Silence.

Well?

Reiss Nothing.

Trauner Nothing at all, sir.

Teacher Then why are you picking on him?

Trauner shrugs.

Why are they picking on you, Feuerbach?

Feuerbach Don't know, sir.

Teacher No reason, eh? So is it true what God says in the Bible: the imagination of man's heart is evil from his youth?

Trauner There is no God.

Teacher Oh, yes, of course, thank you, Trauner, I'd forgotten. Close the window, the rain's coming in. And settle down.

Trauner closes the window. The Teacher fetches the exercise books out of his briefcase. He hands the majority of them to one of the boys for distribution, but retains three of them for specific comment. Before this, however, he decides to pursue his train of thought.

You five bullies ought to be thoroughly ashamed of yourselves. Are you?

He looks at Trauner, who stares back at him impassively.

Evidently not. Well, you should be.

He holds out the first of the exercise books. As he calls their names, the pupils step up to collect their books.

Bauer. You don't have to cover every square inch of the paper. That line down the left-hand side of the page is what we call a margin, it's there for a reason. And there are useful devices known as paragraphs, look in any book, you'll soon get the hang of it.

Bauer Yes, sir.

He takes the book, bows and goes back to his seat.

Teacher Ziegler. You really have to do something about your spelling. The word 'colonies', for example, was in the title I put up, there's no excuse for getting that wrong in so many different ways.

Ziegler No, sir.

He bows and returns to his seat.

Teacher And, finally, Neumann.

Otto Neumann approaches, a pedantic-looking boy with a savage haircut, slightly overweight. The Teacher opens the exercise book and finds his place.

At the end of your essay you say: 'As for the niggers, it really doesn't matter whether they live or die.'

Neumann Yes, sir.

Teacher You shouldn't say things like that. After all, Africans are human beings as well, aren't they?

Neumann doesn't answer, but a flicker of disgust crosses his face. He bows, turns and moves back to his seat. The Teacher looks as if he's about to say something else, but thinks better of it.

Lights down on the classroom. The Teacher steps forward to address the audience.

I didn't want to go home that evening for some reason, felt rather gloomy. So I ducked into a cinema: of course, the newsreel was full of those buffoons in uniform, shouting out their cretinous slogans and marching up and down going nowhere; which made me even gloomier. The feature, an American gangster picture, consisted of people blazing away at each other for ninety minutes in order to prove that good always triumphs. Afterwards, I needed a drink.

THREE

A dingy bar.

The Teacher carries a glass of schnapps back to a small table. No sooner has he sat down, than Nelly, a young blonde prostitute, joins him. A pianist tinkles away in a dark corner.

Nelly On your own?

Teacher Afraid so.

Nelly Is it all right if I join you?

Teacher No.

Nelly moves off, affronted. The Teacher knocks back his schnapps. A shadow falls across his table. He looks up to see an extraordinary figure: a man of about sixty, a former colleague, a roguish, somewhat dishevelled character wearing a leather jacket and an enormous silver tiepin in the shape of a skull. For some reason, he's known as Julius Caesar. He's holding two glasses of schnapps, one of which he puts down in front of the Teacher as he joins him at the table.

Caesar Don't like to see you drinking alone.

Teacher Julius Caesar! How are you?

By way of response, Caesar activates a device in his pocket, which causes one of the skull's eyes to light up red. Then he grins, broadly.

I see.

Caesar So why are you drinking alone?

Teacher I'm depressed by my pupils.

Caesar Why's that?

Teacher I don't so much mind that they piss on everything that's sacred to me. I mind that they piss on it without knowing the first thing about it. I mind that they don't even want to know the first thing about it. In fact, they detest knowledge. They can't bear the idea of having their own opinions. There's a plague spreading; and their souls are covered in huge black boils.

Caesar You want me to explain it to you?

Teacher Can you?

Caesar I had plenty of time to think about all this while I was in jail. I know no one believes I didn't know she was under age; let's just say I didn't have time to go and look her up in the school register. Anyway, it was good to have some time for reflection, and this is what I worked out: me, you and your pupils are three different generations. For boys, there is no more important time than adolescence . . .

Teacher Is this going to take a long time?

Caesar No. Drink your drink and listen. Now, when I was an adolescent, by far the main problem was women: I'm talking about the total unavailability of women. Our only way out was masturbation. When you were an adolescent, by contrast, all the men were away at the front, so women were easy to come by, were they not?

Teacher I suppose so.

Caesar There was something disillusioning and shaming about this, which made you yearn for something you couldn't define – the purity, did you but know it, of masturbation.

Teacher You're completely fixated on sex.

Caesar As for the third generation, your pupils, the woman problem has simply disappeared.

Teacher And why is that?

Caesar Because there aren't any women any more. Just a lot of monsters with rucksacks marching and rowing and chanting slogans and doing gymnastics for the Fatherland. You could call it nihilism if they weren't too stupid to have a single thought of any kind.

Teacher You're exaggerating.

Caesar I'm not. There are cold times coming, the age of the fish.

Teacher The fish?

Caesar Do you know your astrology?

Teacher No.

Caesar The age of Pisces, the age of the fish. People's souls will become cold and unmoving. Every crime – murder, arson, betrayal: they won't only become commonplace, as they are now, they'll actually be encouraged. How can anything be wrong, if it benefits the race?

Teacher That's what they say on the radio.

Caesar Precisely.

Silence. Both men throw back their drinks. Then Julius Caesar surges to his feet, cheerful again.

Come join us at our table. We're all dinosaurs from previous ages.

The Teacher smiles and rises to his feet. But, as the lights go down on the bar, he peels off to speak to the audience.

Teacher Well, one thing led to another and the next morning I woke up in a strange bed with a woman whose name I couldn't for the life of me remember. This meant that when I was summoned to see the headmaster later that morning, I was not at the top of my form.

FOUR

The Headmaster's study. The Headmaster, a benevolent-looking, white-haired party, sits behind his desk. Opposite him, at an angle, is Herr Neumann, the baker, wearing his best suit, shoes ostentatiously gleaming. The Teacher arrives.

Headmaster Ah, come in. Sorry to drag you out of your classroom, but it is rather a serious matter. This is Herr Neumann, Otto's father.

Teacher Very pleased to meet you.

He extends a hand which Herr Neumann conspicuously declines to accept. Instead, he rises ominously to his feet.

Herr Neumann Yesterday afternoon my son Otto informed me that you had made, in the classroom, a most outrageous assertion . . .

Teacher I?

Herr Neumann That's right.

Teacher When was this?

Herr Neumann At the beginning of the geography lesson. Apparently you said to my son Otto in the context of a discussion of our colonial project, 'Negroes are human beings as well.' You understand what I'm saying?

Teacher No, I don't.

Herr Neumann draws himself up, his face flushing with righteous indignation.

Herr Neumann Did you or did you not, in front of your class, utter this indefensible remark on the subject of Negroes?

Teacher I think I said Africans.

Herr Neumann Have you any idea how subversive it is to hold an opinion of this kind about Negroes? It's tantamount to sabotage! Of the Fatherland! And don't you look at me like that! I know you humanists will stop at nothing to poison innocent children with your wicked beliefs!

Teacher Doesn't it say in the Bible that all men are human, no matter what their race?

Herr Neumann Don't quote the Bible at me! You know perfectly well the Bible is nothing but metaphor! At the time it was written, there was no colonial question! It's no good trying to hide behind religion!

Headmaster Herr Neumann, thank you, I believe your point is well taken. I've explained to Herr Neumann that we do have an internal memo, number, um, 5679, of which paragraph 33 states that we take full responsibility for maintaining and in no way undermining the military ideals currently upheld by the State. In that sense, I believe my colleague's statement was unfortunately phrased, for which we apologise unreservedly and thank you for drawing our attention to a lapse which will not be repeated. Good morning, Herr Neumann!

Herr Neumann frowns, inclined for a moment to resist his dismissal. But he contents himself with glowering at the Teacher on his way out.

Herr Neumann We'll be watching every move you make.

He leaves. The Headmaster turns to the Teacher, spreads his hands and shrugs his shoulders.

Headmaster What can you do?

Teacher Yes.

Headmaster I hope you won't take it amiss if I warn you to make sure nothing like this happens again.

Teacher I think I understand.

Headmaster No doubt you're surprised to hear me, who used to be, if I may so express it, a militantly peace-loving man, appearing to sound the trumpets of war.

Teacher I know you do what has to be done.

Headmaster I could defy the spirit of the age and stand up against our baker friend, Herr Neumann: but I would far rather draw my pension.

Teacher I see.

Headmaster I don't want you to think I'm entirely cynical. I am to some extent responding to the spirit of the age. It's a plebeian spirit; but if you've lived long enough, you do begin to acquire a sense of realism.

Silence. The Teacher half turns towards the door.

Teacher Well, if that's . . .

Headmaster There is just one other thing. Please sit down.

The Teacher does so: the Headmaster rises and moves around his desk, handing the Teacher a piece of paper.

I received this this morning. Your class has petitioned me to replace you.

The Teacher reads the piece of paper, shocked.

Signed, as you will see, by every boy in the class.

The Teacher looks up, angry.

Teacher Well, if that's the way of it, I too would like to be assigned to a different class.

Headmaster You think the others will be any better?

The Teacher looks at him, at a loss.

No. Surrender is not the answer. Come with me. I'll show you how to deal with this kind of thing.

The Headmaster strides purposefully out of the room. The Teacher turns to address the audience.

Teacher He put on a magnificent performance in front of the class, ranting and raving, had they all taken leave of their senses, how dare they have the insolence to ask for another teacher, et cetera and so on. All very well for you, I was thinking, you just have to make your speech and go, I'm the one who actually has to stay and teach them. And they were looking at me with such hatred, especially that little monster, Neumann; he's your mortal enemy, I thought, he'll do anything to destroy you, he and his type, I thought, all they want is to wipe out the memory that anyone like you ever existed. Well, I do exist, my young friends; and I have no intention of letting you put me out on the street to starve. I was right, of course I was, to say Africans are human beings: I don't believe I could say as much for these miserable little bastards.

Blackout.

FIVE

Open landscape. Mountains in the distance. Across the stage march the boys from the Teacher's class, dressed in Pioneer uniform, led by a portly Sergeant in his sixties, all singing a patriotic song, 'Ich hatt' einen Kameraden', perhaps, or even the 'Horst Wessel Lied'. They pass on into the distance, still singing; and the Teacher appears, dressed now for the country.

Teacher The worst of it was I couldn't even get away from them over Easter. Thanks to one of those innumerable ludicrous new laws, we were all obliged to spend ten days together at camp, a six-hour drive away in the mountains, the boys and a kindly old sergeant with glasses, who shared my tent and snored the place down. I must say, though, it was good to be out of the city – and the first day I went off for a walk on my own and saw something rather interesting. At the bottom of the hill, in the garden in front of a small cottage, an old woman was standing, waving a stick, shouting 'Who's there? Who's there?' Watching her were two boys of about twelve and a very striking girl of, say, sixteen, wearing a pink blouse. One of the boys suddenly darted through the open door into the cottage; and by this point I'd worked out what was going on. The woman was blind and she was being robbed. I set off down the hill at a run, shouting; all hell broke loose; the girl knocked the old woman over; the boy came running out of the cottage with a jug and a loaf of bread; they all ran for it and I helped the old lady up, who by now was swearing like a trooper. She said there were gangs of these under-age thieves roaming the countryside and they all ought to be rooted up like weeds.

I met the local priest the day I arrived; he told me he'd just taken delivery of the new wine and invited me round to sample it with him. He seemed a cheery enough fellow and I went with him through the village, past the abandoned sawmill which, this time last year, had provided employment for most of the villagers, until the directors and shareholders of the corporation that owned it decided the profit margins were too narrow. Most of the small terraced houses we passed had a child or two sitting in the window painting or otherwise embellishing dolls and toys, piecework, said the priest (who by now was walking quite fast and not making eye-contact with any of the pale, sullen-looking children), miserably paid, but all they could find at the moment. He showed me to his very comfortable study in his very tidy rectory and went to fetch the wine.

SIX

The Priest's study, very comfortable, as described, with a painting on the wall of the Crucifixion, with a Roman centurion in the foreground, looking up at the Cross, as the storm rages and the veil of the Temple is rent. The Priest, a genial-looking, round-faced man, takes a couple of good mouthfuls of wine. The Teacher is looking up at the painting.

Teacher My parents have that very painting on their wall.

Priest Really?

Teacher I often used to think about that centurion at the foot of the Cross. When he was retired, back in Italy perhaps, everyone around him going on about how perfect and everlasting the Roman Empire was, and he knowing all along its days were numbered.

Priest Yes.

Teacher If there are only a few sane people left in a country, how do they go about putting the overwhelming majority into straitjackets?

Priest What is it you teach?

Teacher History and geography. From which I conclude that the earth may be round, but history has some pretty sharp corners.

Silence. The Priest offers the Teacher a cake, which he accepts, then replaces the plate without taking one himself.

Aren't you going to have one?

Priest I don't eat much. Leaves more room for the drink.

He laughs, then abruptly falls silent, his expression changing.

You're thinking about those children, aren't you? Sitting in the windows.

Teacher How did you know?

Priest It's not difficult. They're hard to forget about. One in three of them is malnourished.

The Teacher hesitates, the cake halfway to his mouth.

Your eating that cake doesn't do them any harm, any more than my drinking my wine. No, what's done the damage is the closing of the sawmill.

Teacher Tell me . . .

Priest Yes?

Teacher Why does the Church always side with the rich?

Priest Because it has to.

Teacher Why?

Priest Any given state, whatever political system it adopts, is always controlled by the rich. The rich are always with us. And it's not up to the Church to decree how a state should be ruled. The Church has to support the state, which is to say, the rich.

Teacher Can that be right?

Priest The goal of the state is to provide the greatest happiness for the greatest number. It's the Church's duty to support that goal.

Teacher You're not trying to tell me it's the goal of our present state to provide happiness?

Priest Pascal says: 'We search for happiness and find only misery and death.'

Teacher Does he?

Priest I expect you're surprised to find a simple country priest quoting Pascal. The fact is, I'm not a simple country priest. This is what we call a punishment posting. Yes. Of course if it weren't for the world's little stupidities, we'd none of us be here in the first place.

He smiles ruefully and refills their glasses.

A state is an expression of man's free will, and therefore part of the will of God.

Teacher Suppose the state disintegrates?

Priest A state never disintegrates, it just replaces one system with another.

Teacher And the Church supports it no matter what? It always supports the sawmill-owners rather than the children painting dolls in the window?

Priest Yes.

Teacher But why?

Priest Because the rich always win.

Teacher Call that morality?

Priest Morality consists in accurate thinking. Naturally the rich will always win because they're more brutal, more ruthless and more unscrupulous. Haven't you read that it's easier for a camel to pass through the eye of a needle than for a rich man to enter Heaven?

Teacher Then how is the Church going to pass through the eye of the needle?

Priest The Church *is* the eye of the needle.

Pause. The Teacher, bested, reflects for a moment.

Teacher So the Church never fights on behalf of the poor?

Priest The Church does fight for the poor. It fights for everyone. On different fronts.

Teacher You mean, on the spiritual front?

Priest The spiritual front has its victims too.

Teacher Such as?

Priest Christ.

He refills the Teacher's glass.

Teacher Those children, you know. The reason they don't speak to you in the street is not because they hate you: it's because they're hungry.

Priest And because they no longer believe in God.

Teacher How can you expect them to?

Priest God moves through every street.

Teacher Then why doesn't He do something to help those children?

Silence. The Priest empties his glass.

Priest Because God is the most terrible thing in the world. Because he's punishing us.

Teacher What for?

Priest Exercising our free will.

Teacher I don't believe that.

Priest Then you can't believe in God.

Teacher You're right: I don't.

The Priest says nothing, pours himself another glass of wine.

I grew up during the Great War. How could you come out of that believing in God?

Priest I did.

Pause.

Teacher The Greeks got by all right without all that free will and original sin.

Priest One of the earliest Greek philosophers, Anaximander, sixth century BC, said: 'Fate decrees that everything must return to its origins; where it must pay for the guilt of its existence in punishment and suffering.'

Teacher All right then, I exercise my free will by refusing to believe in God.

SEVEN

The camp ground. A couple of tents visible. The Teacher sits at a trestle table.

Teacher Since I'd seen that there were thieves about, the sergeant and I decided to post sentries at night. I took the first watch. It was a beautiful moonlit night and I was happy to be away from the sergeant's snoring. I was by the haystack at the top end of the camp when I saw a figure flitting out of the woods. It was a young boy. He went straight up to Robert Ziegler, who was guarding the northern perimeter, spoke to him briefly, handed him something and disappeared. It was some kind of a letter. Ziegler looked around, glanced at the letter and stuffed it in his pocket. Thinking about it later, it seemed to me the young boy might have been one of the gang who had robbed the old lady. I decided not to say a word to anyone.

The next day I was told there had been a disturbance in one of the tents, Ziegler's, as it turned out, which he shared with the repellent Otto Neumann and another boy called Heinrich Reiss. I asked the sergeant to send them to me one by one, Ziegler last.

Heinrich Reiss, one of the smaller boys, makes his way to stand in front of the trestle table. The Teacher studies him as he waits, increasingly uneasy.

Well, Reiss, what seems to be going on?

Reiss It's Neumann and Ziegler, sir, they never stop quarrelling.

Teacher Oh, I see, nothing to do with you at all?

Reiss No, sir; I was going to ask if I might be transferred to a different tent.

Teacher What is it they quarrel about?

Reiss Everything, sir. And it's always Neumann who starts it.

Teacher Is it, now?

Reiss He's a pain in the arse, sir.

Teacher Thank you, Reiss, that'll do.

As Reiss leaves and Neumann enters, we become dimly aware of another boy upstage, watching. Neumann's expression is mutinous, flushed with his father's righteous indignation.

What's this constant quarrelling I keep hearing about?

Neumann It's Ziegler, sir, he won't let me get to sleep. He's always lighting his candle in the middle of the night.

Teacher Why would that be?

Neumann Writing a lot of rubbish.

Teacher Writing?

Neumann Yes, sir.

Teacher Letters? Epic poems?

Neumann No, sir. His diary.

Teacher A diary.

Neumann Yes, it's stupid.

Teacher Not necessarily.

Neumann looks up at the Teacher, his expression withering.

Neumann A diary is a typical sign of the overvaluing of the individual ego.

Teacher You hear that on the radio?

Neumann Yes, sir.

Teacher And have you read this diary?

Neumann No, sir, he keeps it locked up in a tin box.

Teacher I see. Is your father well?

Neumann Er, yes, sir.

Teacher That's all, thank you.

Neumann leaves and Ziegler enters. The upstage figure hasn't moved.

Ziegler.

Ziegler Yes, sir.

Teacher Why are you always quarrelling with Neumann?

Ziegler Because he's an arsehole, sir, everybody thinks so.

Teacher Be that as it may . . .

Ziegler He can't bear anyone being at all reflective or private. It drives him crazy. I keep a diary in a locked box and he keeps trying to break into the box and grab it.

Teacher So what do you do?

Ziegler Push him off. Sleep with the box. When I have to be out, I hide it in my sleeping bag.

Teacher And what do you do in this diary, describe your experiences?

Ziegler That's right, sir.

Teacher All of them?

Ziegler Well . . . yes, sir.

Teacher Thank you, Ziegler, that will be all.

As Ziegler leaves, the Teacher suddenly gets up and pounces, dragging out Dieter Trauner, who's been eavesdropping behind the tent.

What are you doing, Trauner?

Trauner Nothing, sir.

Teacher Well, will you go and do nothing somewhere else?

Trauner Yes, sir.

Teacher And the next time I catch you doing nothing within earshot of me, I shall ask the sergeant to let you do nothing for a whole afternoon in detention, is that clear?

Trauner Yes, sir.

Teacher On your way.

Trauner hurries off. The Teacher turns to the audience. Light change.

As soon as the sergeant led them all off for afternoon manoeuvres, I headed straight for the tent.

He throws back the flap of the tent and steps into it. He picks up a letter.

The first thing I found was a letter from the ghastly Neumann's mother telling him to be sure to report me immediately if I made any more subversive remarks 'like the one about the niggers'.

He replaces the letter, fumbles around in one of the sleeping bags and brings out a tin box. He pulls over a camp-stool and makes himself comfortable.

Then I came up with the famous box.

The box is locked. The Teacher produces a piece of wire; and after some manipulation the lock gives. He opens the box and brings out a book bound in green leather. As he opens it, a scrap of paper flutters to the ground.

Ah. Here was the letter he'd been handed in the night. It said: 'Can't come today. Two a.m. tomorrow. – Eva.'

He looks up, intrigued.

Eva.

He thinks for a moment, then looks down and opens the diary, begins to leaf through it.

Ziegler's spelling still left a great deal to be desired. Otherwise there was nothing very remarkable in the diary, all conventional enough. Until I got to yesterday's entry. This described how, the previous afternoon on manoeuvres, Ziegler had managed to get himself lost in the woods. He was wandering about hopelessly, near the cliffs, when he suddenly came face to face with a girl in a pink blouse. She agreed to show him the way out of the woods.

EIGHT

Light change. The Teacher remains where he is, reading the diary; but at the same time, we are now somewhere up in the hills, at the edge of the woods. The girl, Eva, in her pink blouse and dark, ragged skirt, barefoot, leads Ziegler to the side of the hill and points downwards.

Eva There it is, down there. You can find your own way from here.

Ziegler Thank you. Without you, I could have been in the woods for days.

Silence. They seem mysteriously reluctant to part.

Can I ask you a question?

Eva Maybe.

Ziegler You said you lived up by the cliffs. The map doesn't show any houses up there.

Eva Doesn't it?

Ziegler I expect the map's wrong.

Eva I don't live in a house.

Another silence.

Ziegler Well . . .

Eva Listen.

Ziegler Yes?

Eva Will you promise not to tell anyone you met me?

Ziegler Well . . .

Eva I'll give you a kiss if you promise.

Ziegler Why don't you want anyone to know?

Eva I don't, that's all.

Ziegler All right, then.

She steps over to him and gives him a quick peck on the cheek. He takes hold of her arm.

Wait a minute, that doesn't count.

Eva What do you mean?

Ziegler It only counts if it's a kiss on the mouth.

After the briefest hesitation, Eva puts a hand round the back of Ziegler's head and kisses him on the mouth. It's a long kiss, which gives every sign of being pleasurable: until, suddenly, Ziegler abruptly breaks away.

Pig!

Eva What?

Ziegler You put your tongue in my mouth.

Eva So?

Ziegler It's disgusting!

Eva Is it?

She grabs him and kisses him again, once again putting her tongue in his mouth. He struggles for a moment, then pushes her violently away. They glare at each other for a few seconds, then Ziegler turns on his heel and begins to move away. Eva grabs up a stone and throws it at his head, narrowly missing. He turns back to her, appalled.

Ziegler What did you do that for?

Eva Felt like it.

Ziegler You could have killed me.

Eva Wouldn't have lost any sleep over it.

Ziegler You'd have been hanged.

Eva Probably will be, anyway.

Strange silence.

Come here.

After the briefest hesitation, Ziegler obeys. She grabs him and kisses him again. A moment later, he breaks away again, flushed with anger.

Ziegler You did it again!

Eva You'll get used to it in the end.

Ziegler grabs up a branch and swipes at her. She puts her arms up to defend her head, but otherwise makes no attempt to escape, half turning her back to him. Ziegler hits her a few more times around the back and shoulders. Suddenly, she collapses. Alarmed, Ziegler approaches; he prods at her cautiously with the branch. No reaction.

Ziegler Are you all right?

No response. He drops the branch, genuinely concerned now. Then, it seems to dawn on him what's going on. He kneels beside Eva's body. Gingerly he starts, very slowly, to pull up her skirt. She's not wearing underwear. He looks down at her. Suddenly, her eyes open.

Eva You're the one could have been hanged.

She pulls him down on top of her.

NINE

Light change. Ziegler and Eva disappear; and the Teacher looks up from his reading of the diary at the sound of the distant bugle. He puts the diary back in its box.

Teacher The last thing he wrote, in capital letters, was: ANYONE WHO TOUCHES MY BOX DIES! Ha. Boys!

As he speaks, he's using his piece of wire to try to work the lock. But as the sounds of marching feet and a military song draw nearer, he has to abandon the attempt.

It was no good. I seemed to have broken the lock.

He gives up, folds away the camp-stool, stows the box back in Ziegler's sleeping bag and moves away from the tent.

Light change. And the Teacher installs himself behind the trestle table.

Before too long, there was the most terrible fracas. Ziegler found his box had been opened and fell on the hapless Neumann. He had to be dragged off him. The sergeant brought them to me.

The Sergeant leads on Ziegler and Neumann, whose nose is still bleeding and whose eye is closing and turning black. The Teacher contemplates him for a moment.

Good heavens, Neumann, what have you been up to?

Sergeant He broke into Ziegler's box, sir.

Neumann I didn't, it wasn't me, sir, it wasn't me!

Ziegler Course it was, who else could it have been, sir?

Neumann You're a liar!

Ziegler He's been threatening to do it all along.

Neumann Yes, but it still wasn't me!

Sergeant Silence!

The boys fall silent for a moment. Then Neumann pipes up.

Neumann Permission to speak, sir.

Teacher Go on.

Neumann I'd like permission to change tents.

Teacher All right.

Neumann I didn't read his diary, sir, honestly, I swear. Please help me, sir!

The Teacher contemplates the abject figure for a moment, trying to suppress his satisfaction.

Teacher I'll do what I can. Thank you, that'll be all.

The Sergeant leads away the two boys; the Teacher watches them go, then turns to the audience.

I suppose I ought to have explained, there and then, that it was I who'd read the diary. But it somehow didn't seem the moment. Then, later in the afternoon, there was more uproar. Somebody's camera had been stolen. That made my mind up. Unless I was much mistaken, Ziegler and Eva had a rendezvous at two a.m. The thing to do was to follow him and confront them both. I'd tell her to return the camera, or I'd take her to the police, and then never show her face again; and then I'd give him a piece of my mind and let him know I was the one who opened the box. Excellent plan. A proper exercise of my free will.

TEN

Two a.m. Moonlight. Edge of the woods. Ziegler waits in a clearing, moving restlessly to and fro. The Teacher waits in the shadows, watching. Suddenly, Eva is there, as if materialising out of nowhere, startling Ziegler. She throws herself into his arms; a long kiss. The Teacher moves forward, poised to intervene: but then Ziegler speaks and the Teacher slips back into the shadows.

Ziegler You smell wonderful.

Eva It's perfume, from the chemist's in the village.

Ziegler Must be expensive.

Eva No, it was free.

She kisses him again.

Getting used to it now?

Ziegler Yes.

Eva What shall we do?

Ziegler hesitates, surprised by the question.

Ziegler Can we make love?

Eva You want to do it every day?

Ziegler If possible.

Eva Won't you think I'm a slut?

Ziegler No, of course not. Why should I think that?

Eva Because I do what you want me to.

Ziegler Nobody's perfect.

He smiles to acknowledge his own joke; then suddenly notices there are tears in Eva's eyes.

What's the matter?

Eva What do you mean?

Ziegler You're crying.

Eva Everything's so difficult.

Ziegler Tell me.

Eva I'm afraid you won't love me any more.

Ziegler Course I will.

Eva I'm an orphan.

Ziegler That's not your fault.

Eva They fostered me but when I was twelve my foster-father kept after me all the time, so I took some money and ran away. They caught me and put me in reform school. I broke out last year and now I live in a cave up in the cliffs with four other kids who got fed up painting dolls. I'm the leader. I have to make sure they're all fed.

Ziegler Is that why you took the camera?

Eva breaks away from him, suddenly suspicious.

It's all right, I'm not going to tell on you.

Eva Don't, you mustn't, they'd send me back to reform school.

Ziegler I wouldn't let them. I'd defend you. I want to stay here with you.

Eva, her back to the audience, swiftly and easily slips out of her clothes. Ziegler kneels in front of her and buries his face in her stomach. She raises him up and sits him on a tree trunk; then she kneels in front of him and starts to undo his shirt buttons. Darkness.

Teacher The moon vanished behind a cloud. I was still trying to decide what to do. Perhaps it would be better to speak to him tomorrow and tell him about the box. It was time for me to leave. Not that I could see a thing. Then, here's what happened: I stretched out my hand and touched a tree. Only it wasn't a tree. It moved. It was somebody's face.

ELEVEN

The camp ground. Sound of rain on canvas. The Teacher moves downstage, pensive. Bugle call.

The next morning I overslept. By the time I was up, ready to have my heart-to-heart with Ziegler, everybody had left for the day's exercise. It was our last full day in the camp.

The boys return, wet from the rain. The Sergeant makes his way over to the Teacher.

Everything all right?

Sergeant Wretched boy Neumann's gone missing.

Teacher Oh?

Sergeant Very misty up there, expect he got lost. Useless article.

He moves off. The Teacher crosses to throw back the flap of the tent, revealing Ziegler, who's writing in his diary.

Teacher Ah, Ziegler, I wanted a word with you.

Ziegler says nothing. His hand has automatically covered the page of his open diary.

Keeping up our diary?

Ziegler Yes, sir.

Teacher You think it was Neumann broke into your box . . .

Ziegler I don't think it, I know it.

Teacher How can you be so sure?

Ziegler He told me himself.

Teacher He told you?

Ziegler He admitted it this morning. He opened it with a piece of wire. Then he couldn't get it shut because he'd broken the lock.

Teacher What else did he say?

Ziegler He asked me to forgive him.

Teacher And?

Ziegler I did.

Teacher You forgave him?

Ziegler Yes.

Teacher Any idea what's happened to Neumann?

Ziegler How should I know? Got lost, I expect. Happened to me the other day.

Teacher Yes, well . . .

He can't think of anything else to say and retreats, lowering the flap of the tent behind him.

Light change. As the Teacher speaks, the boys, in their uniforms, form up facing front under the supervision of the Sergeant.

The next morning two lumberjacks appeared in the camp. They'd found Neumann, face down in a ditch. He was dead as a doornail. I went to identify the body. Somebody had hit him with a rock, which was found nearby, stained with blood, then dragged the body twenty yards and dumped it in the ditch. They also found a pencil and a compass. I made a statement to the public prosecutor and contacted the headmaster. The prosecutor came out to the camp to speak directly to the boys.

The Public Prosecutor, a stout man, formally dressed, stands in front of the gathering of boys, flanked by the Teacher and the Sergeant.

Public Prosecutor I must ask you, boys, if anyone has any information that might throw some light on this dreadful business, or even any suspicions whatsoever, let him speak now.

Silence. Then, timidly, Heinrich Reiss raises his hand.

What is it, my boy? Speak up.

Reiss Sir, Ziegler and Neumann fought all the time, sir. Then Neumann read Ziegler's diary and Ziegler said he'd kill him.

Public Prosecutor Is this true?

Reiss Yes, sir.

Public Prosecutor Which of you is Ziegler?

Ziegler steps out of the ranks and approaches. He lowers his head.

Have you anything to say, Ziegler?

Ziegler raises his head and looks steadfastly at the Public Prosecutor.

Ziegler Yes. I did it.

Blackout.

TWELVE

The courtroom. The trial is presided over by the kindly looking, grandfatherly President of the Juvenile Court and the accused, in the dock, is Robert Ziegler. Also present are the Counsels for the Prosecution and Defence, the latter now on his feet, addressing the court. There are Court officials, reporters in the Press Gallery and, in the witness stand, Herr and Frau Neumann, the Headmaster, the Sergeant, Heinrich Reiss and a heavily veiled woman, Ziegler's mother. Also, of course, the Teacher.

Defence Counsel Ladies and gentlemen, in this sensational murder trial, the defence finds itself in an extremely precarious position, in which it is obliged to conduct its case not only against the Counsel for the Prosecution, but also against the defendant, who has pleaded guilty to this offence. It will be my contention and indeed is my profound conviction that the defendant did not commit this crime. He is shielding someone. I have no doubt that he encountered the victim up by the cliffs; and that they fought. But did the accused then creep up behind Neumann and hit him with a rock? He did not. I repeat: the defendant is shielding someone else. He is guilty of no more than being an accomplice.

A light change, denoting a passage of time. Ziegler is on his feet now, being interrogated by the President.

President Robert Ziegler, you stand accused of murder in the first degree. How do you plead?

Ziegler Guilty.

President Your teacher has stated that he considered you to be one of his brightest pupils.

Ziegler I always thought he was kind of naive.

President Really? In what way?

Ziegler He used to talk about the way things ought to be, rather than the way they actually are.

President I see. Had you some idea of what you wanted to be when you grow up?

Ziegler An inventor.

President Easier said than done, I imagine. Suppose you'd found you weren't able to invent anything?

Ziegler A pilot.

President Do you believe in God?

Ziegler Yes, sir.

President And do you know the fifth commandment?

Ziegler Yes, sir.

President Are you sorry for what you've done?

Silence. Ziegler struggles not to give way to his emotions.

Ziegler Yes, sir. Very sorry.

It doesn't ring true. The President consults his papers for a moment.

President Now. Tell us what happened on the day of the murder.

Ziegler We set out very early. We were supposed to be spread out, advancing towards a range of hills held by the enemy. Near the cliffs I ran into Neumann. I was furious with him for breaking into my box, even though he denied it . . .

President One moment. In his statement to the local magistrate, your teacher said you had told him Neumann admitted breaking into your box.

Ziegler I just made that up.

President Why?

Ziegler So as to divert suspicion.

President I see. Go on.

Ziegler We started fighting, Neumann and I, and he almost pushed me off the cliff. That made me see red, so I jumped up and threw the rock at him.

President You were still on the cliff?

Ziegler Erm, no.

President Where were you, then?

Pause.

Ziegler I can't remember.

President You can't remember where you were when you threw the rock?

Ziegler No, sir.

President Then what is the next thing you do remember?

Ziegler I went back to the camp and wrote in my diary that I'd had a fight with Neumann.

President The sentence is unfinished.

Ziegler Yes, because the teacher interrupted me.

President He wanted to speak to you about something?

Ziegler I don't know, sir.

President No doubt he'll explain it to us.

The President indicates an evidence table, on which lie Ziegler's diary, the rock, a pencil and a compass.

The exhibit on the table there; is that the rock you threw at Neumann?

Ziegler Yes, sir.

President What about the pencil and the compass?

Ziegler No, they're not mine.

President So they were Neumann's?

Ziegler Yes, sir.

The President checks his notes.

President Well, it says here, only the pencil belonged to Neumann.

Ziegler Oh, yes.

President So the compass did belong to you?

Ziegler Yes, sir.

President Then why didn't you say so?

Ziegler Er, I'd forgotten.

The Defence Counsel rises to his feet.

Defence Counsel Your honour . . .

President Yes.

Defence Counsel I suggest the compass did not belong to the defendant.

President Meaning?

Defence Counsel Meaning that the compass very likely belonged neither to Neumann nor to the defendant, but to a third party.

He sits down.

Ziegler There was no third party.

The Defence Counsel springs to his feet again.

Defence Counsel I should like to know how the defendant remembers this so clearly, when he seems to have forgotten all the other circumstances surrounding the incident.

The Prosecuting Counsel is on his feet now.

Prosecuting Counsel My learned friend apparently seeks to make the familiar suggestion that it was not his client who committed the murder, but some Great Unknown . . .

Defence Counsel As the Court knows, there is a girl involved, a convicted felon, leader of a gang of juvenile criminals; I would hardly describe her as a Great Unknown . . .

Prosecuting Counsel This girl has already been thoroughly questioned and denies any involvement: whereas the accused has made a very straightforward confession. The suggestion that he is shielding someone seems to be entirely fanciful.

The Defence Counsel turns to Ziegler.

Defence Counsel There is an entry in your diary, is there not, which reads . . . (*He consults a piece of paper.*) 'She threw a stone at me, which could have killed me.'

Ziegler I was exaggerating. It was a very small stone.

Defence Counsel Was it?

Ziegler Please don't defend me, sir. I want to be punished for what I've done!

Defence Counsel Have you no consideration for your mother? She's sitting here, in court. Have you any idea what you're putting her through?

Ziegler turns to look at her. She's invisible behind her veil. Ziegler lowers his head, ashamed.

THIRTEEN

Lights down on the courtroom. The Teacher moves downstage to speak to the audience.

Teacher During the lunch break, I stepped into a tobacconist's to buy some cigarettes and something very curious happened. The shop was run by an old couple; they didn't have the right change and while the old woman stepped across the street to get some, the old man started to talk about the trial. He blamed everyone involved, including the teacher, i.e. me. In his view the root cause of the problem was that everybody involved – teachers, parents, boys – behaved as if God no longer existed. In the course of the conversation I'd had with the priest, up in the mountain village, I'd told him I didn't believe in God. Since then, I'd begun to think perhaps there was a God: a very cruel, capricious and cold God. Now, as the old man rambled on about how everything was going to rack and ruin, I suddenly heard, very clearly, a voice. It said: 'When you're called as a witness and take my name, you'd better tell them it was you who broke into the box.' 'But I'll get into trouble,' I said, silently, 'I'll lose my job.' 'So be it,' the voice said.

FOURTEEN

Back in the courtroom. Frau Ziegler is in the witness box, still wearing her veil. Her voice is somewhat harsh and grating.

President You say your son has a harsh temper?

Frau Ziegler He inherited it from his late father.

President How long ago, may I ask, did your husband die?

Frau Ziegler Ten years. Your Honour, do you mind if I ask my son a question?

President Please, go ahead.

Frau Ziegler steps down into the well of the court, moves to the evidence table, picks up the compass and turns to Ziegler.

Frau Ziegler Since when have you had a compass?

Ziegler, taken by surprise, says nothing for a moment.

You've never had one. We had a quarrel about it the day before you went off to the camp. You said you were the only boy in your class who didn't have a compass.

She turns triumphantly to the President and hands him the compass.

It's not his, Your Honour.

A murmur ripples through the courtroom.

President Answer your mother's question.

Ziegler My mother's a liar.

Frau Ziegler A liar?

Ziegler Yes.

Frau Ziegler How dare you? I have never told a lie in my life! Whereas you've always been a chronic liar! I'm telling the truth and you're just trying to protect this whore!

Ziegler She's not a whore.

Frau Ziegler Oh, yes, she is. All you ever think about is that miserable bitch, you never spare a thought for your poor mother!

Ziegler She's a far better person than you'll ever be!

The President, suddenly furious, raps his gavel and intervenes.

President Silence! You are sentenced to two days' imprisonment for contempt of court! Now behave yourself! I must say, it's extremely revealing, that you're capable of speaking to your mother like that.

Ziegler She's no mother! She's never given a damn about me!

President That's enough!

He turns to Frau Ziegler.

Thank you very much, Frau Ziegler, you're excused.

Light change, denoting a time-lapse. The Teacher is now in the witness box. Eva is now present in the courtroom, sitting next to a uniformed female Warder.

The victim's father, Herr Neumann, referred in his testimony to an incident in which you clashed with the deceased in class on the subject of Negroes.

Teacher Africans, yes.

President Tell us more about this.

Teacher I merely pointed out to Otto Neumann, who, it seemed to me, had expressed himself rather intemperately on the subject, that the Bible enjoins us to be charitable towards all our fellow-creatures.

President So you bore no grudge against the deceased?

Teacher None whatsoever. Your Honour, I wonder if I may offer some, I think, relevant information.

President By all means.

Teacher The defendant's box, in which he kept his diary: it was not Otto Neumann who broke into it.

President Not Otto Neumann? Then who was it?

Teacher Me. I opened it with a piece of wire.

Uproar in the court. Ziegler stares at the Teacher, his mouth open. The President drops his pencil. As he fumbles to reclaim it, the sound dies to a murmur. Both Counsels are on their feet.

President You?

Teacher Yes, sir.

Prosecuting Counsel But why?

Teacher Curiosity. Then, when the trouble started, I didn't speak up for entirely cowardly reasons. I had intended to discuss the matter privately with Ziegler later, but was overtaken by events.

Silence. The Prosecuting Counsel takes a moment to assimilate this; then he continues, his expression grave.

Prosecuting Counsel You must be aware, sir, that this revelation exposes you to the possibility of indictment for, at the very least, withholding of evidence and for being an accessory to robbery.

Teacher I believe I swore to tell the whole truth.

Time-lapse, indicated by a light change. Now Eva is in the witness box. The President holds up the compass.

President Do you know what this is?

Eva It tells you what direction to go in.

President Do you know who it belongs to?

Eva Not me. I think I do know, though.

President I hope you're not trying to mislead the Court.

Eva looks across the courtroom and, for a moment, locks eyes with the Teacher. Then she turns back to the President.

Eva No, sir. I want to tell the truth, like the teacher.

President I see. Go on, then.

Eva I met Ziegler near the cave where I was living. Then Neumann turned up.

President You were present?

Eva Yes, sir.

President Why didn't you tell us this before? You mean to say all the way through the preliminary examination you were lying when you said you didn't witness Ziegler's assault on Neumann?

Eva No, sir. Ziegler never assaulted Neumann.

President Then what happened?

Eva They had a terrible fight; then Neumann pushed Ziegler over the cliff. I thought he'd killed him, I was furious, so I picked up the rock and ran after him. I was going to hit him on the head, that's what I wanted to do, but suddenly this boy I didn't know jumped out of the undergrowth, snatched the rock out of my hand and ran after Neumann. I saw him catch up with him. They started talking. He was still holding the rock. I was scared they'd both come back to get me, so I hid. But they set off in a different direction, Neumann in front. Then suddenly the other boy lifted the rock and brought it down on Neumann's head. Neumann went down like a skittle. Then the other boy dragged him away and tipped him into the ditch. He didn't know I was watching. I ran back to the cliff and found Ziegler. He wasn't hurt, except for a few scratches . . .

The Defence Counsel is on his feet now; he interrupts her.

Defence Counsel I should like to make a formal request, Your Honour, that the charges against my client, Robert Ziegler, be dropped immediately.

President Just a moment, Counsellor, how do we know what this person is saying is the truth?

Ziegler It is.

The President turns to him.

President Are you saying you too witnessed this assault? By this mystery assailant?

The Defence Counsel turns to Eva.

Defence Counsel It was you who attacked Otto Neumann, wasn't it?

Eva No, sir.

President Can you explain why you have concealed this information until today?

Eva Ziegler took the blame because he was sure it was me who killed Neumann. He refused to believe it was somebody else.

President And yet you expect us to believe it?

Eva I don't know, sir. But that's what happened.

President And you would have sat calmly by and watched an innocent boy sentenced?

Eva Not calmly, sir; but I was afraid you'd send me back to reform school. Anyway, I've told you now, he's not guilty.

President Why have you waited until now?

Eva I think it was because the teacher told the truth.

Prosecuting Counsel Extraordinary!

President Suppose the teacher hadn't told the truth?

Eva I wouldn't have either.

Defence Counsel I was under the impression you were in love with Ziegler.

Pause. Eva looks at Ziegler for a moment; then back at the Defence Counsel.

Eva No, sir.

Ziegler rises to his feet.

I never loved him.

Ziegler sits down again, devastated.

President Very well. So you admit you picked up the rock and followed Neumann?

Eva Yes, sir.

President With the intention of killing him?

Eva I don't know, sir. Anyway, I didn't.

President What did you do?

Eva I told you, this stranger appeared, pushed me over and ran after Neumann with the rock in his hand.

President Can you describe this stranger?

Eva Everything happened so quickly . . .

Prosecuting Counsel I said as much: the Great Unknown!

President Would you recognise him again?

Eva Maybe. He had big, stary eyes, like a fish.

Lights down on the courtroom. The Teacher, who has leapt to his feet, moves downstage, fast.

Teacher As soon as she said those words, I knew who it was. A fish in the age of the fish. The next day I waited for him on his way out of school and invited him to join me for an ice cream.

FIFTEEN

An ice-cream parlour. The Teacher sits at a table with Dieter Trauner, watching him dig into a large lemon-and-strawberry sorbet.

Teacher Good?

Trauner Very.

Teacher Have you been following the case?

Trauner Oh, yes, sir. I'm glad they found Ziegler not guilty.

Teacher Well, he was found guilty of being an accessory to robbery.

Trauner Suspended sentence, sir. Better than being found guilty of murder.

Teacher And the girl's been indicted for first-degree murder, what do you think about that?

Trauner Just as it should be.

Teacher So you don't think it was one of the other boys?

Trauner Of course not. She made that up, trying to lie her way out of it.

He frowns and puts his spoon down.

What exactly is it you want from me, sir?

Teacher I thought, Trauner, you might have some idea who the other boy was.

Trauner Me? Why?

Teacher You recall I caught you spying that day in the camp? And I remember that morning in class, the way you were watching the others beat up Feuerbach.

Trauner Yes. I've always liked to watch.

Teacher Well, I thought you might have seen something.

Trauner No.

Teacher Did you read Ziegler's diary?

Trauner No.

He picks up his spoon and takes another mouthful of sorbet.

But I did follow you that night when you went and spied on Ziegler and the girl.

Teacher Did you?

Trauner I was standing behind you. You touched my face. You were terrified.

He smiles mirthlessly.

I wasn't.

Teacher Did you like Neumann?

Trauner Very much.

Teacher So why . . . ?

He breaks off. Trauner looks at him for a moment, narrowing his prominent eyes.

Trauner You're talking to me as if you think I killed Neumann. But that's impossible. The girl said whoever it was had eyes like a fish. I have eyes like a deer, my mother's always saying; and everyone agrees.

The Teacher suppresses a smile.

Did I say something funny? As a matter of fact, sir, you're the one who has eyes like a fish.

Teacher Me?

Trauner Yes. That's actually your nickname at school. The fish. Didn't you know that?

Teacher I didn't.

Trauner Yes, because you have such an expressionless face. No one can ever tell what you're thinking. We always say if someone was run over in the street, you wouldn't help, you'd just stand there watching, with those big, fishy eyes . . .

His expression suddenly changes: for a moment he looks frightened. Then his spoon clatters down on his plate.

Thank you very much for the ice, sir, I'd better go home now, I don't want to be in trouble for being late. Do you think they'll let you come back to the school after what you've done, sir? I wouldn't have thought so. Goodbye.

He hurries away. Blackout.

SIXTEEN

The Teacher's room. Across the table in the window, reaching down to the floor, is an enormous Nazi banner. The Teacher perches on the corner of the table, facing the audience.

Teacher The next day happened to be the birthday of the Great Arsehole who, for the moment, was our leader.

I'd been supplied with a banner to hang out of my window and I thought about not bothering or even defacing it. But that would have been stupid. If you're surrounded by the criminally insane, you have to behave like an insane criminal, especially when the trait most prized by these lying halfwits is craven conformism. So, out it goes.

With some difficulty, he bundles the banner out of the window.

The main disadvantage of this was that I would have to leave the window open, thus being unable to avoid the moronic repetitive songs of the divisions of impressionable nincompoops marching by under the command of total idiots.

Indeed, the sound of Nazi anthems is now audible and continues throughout the scene.

Yes, yet again I toed the line. Better fed than dead!

A knock at the door. Surprised, the Teacher goes over to open it, and lets in one of his pupils, Franz Bauer, who comes into the room and bows to the Teacher.

Bauer. What a surprise. What can I do for you?

Bauer It's about the compass, sir.

Teacher Yes?

Bauer I read about the compass they found next to Neumann's body.

Teacher And?

Bauer I know who it belonged to.

Teacher Who?

Bauer Trauner.

Teacher Aha. How do you know?

Bauer We shared a tent, sir. He was looking for it everywhere.

Teacher You think Trauner might have had something to do with the murder?

Silence. Bauer looks away.

You think he was capable of doing such a thing?

Bauer I think anyone's capable of anything.

Teacher Including murder?

Bauer Why not?

Teacher But why should Trauner have murdered Neumann? What would be his motive?

Bauer He was always saying how stupid Neumann was.

Teacher That's hardly a motive. I mean . . .

He gestures at the window, through which float the sounds of singing and brass bands.

Bauer Trauner is insatiably curious, he always wants to know everything about everything. He once told me he'd like to watch someone die.

Teacher What?

Bauer He said he'd like to watch the way it happened. He also told me he'd like to watch a baby being born.

The Teacher moves over to the window, thinking about this. He looks down at the parade, below.

Teacher Shouldn't you be down there marching?

Bauer I said I wasn't feeling well.

Teacher Your secret's safe with me.

Bauer I know that.

He moves over to join the Teacher at the window.

I couldn't face it. All those people shouting orders. And then, to cap it all, those dreary speeches.

Teacher I hope no one else in the class thinks that way.

Bauer There's four of us.

Teacher Really?

Bauer You remember that petition we all signed asking the headmaster to replace you? I only signed because they made me. Afterwards, I found there were three others who felt the same, who knew you were right about the Africans.

Teacher Is that so?

Bauer We've formed a club. We meet in secret once a week. To talk about the way things ought to be.

Teacher Ziegler accused me of doing that, in court.

Bauer Well, you do, sir. That's why we like you. That's why I came to talk all this over with you. We decided, yesterday, when we were discussing the way you told them about the box. We all think you're the only adult we know who has any respect for the truth.

Silence. A thought strikes the Teacher.

Teacher Tell me, Bauer, is it true my nickname is 'the fish'?

Bauer Who told you that?

Teacher Trauner.

Bauer It's not true. You have a completely different nickname.

Teacher What is it?

Bauer hesitates. Then, he grins.

Bauer 'The Nigger'.

They both laugh. Then Bauer's expression becomes serious.

Sir, do you think Trauner is the murderer?

Teacher Yes, I think he is.

Bauer I do, too. We're going to go to work at the club, we'll put a watch on him and we'll get that girl acquitted.

Teacher Start by telling them what you know about the compass.

Bauer We will, sir.

Teacher Do you have a motto at your club?

Bauer 'Truth and Justice'

Teacher So that's where they've gone.

He smiles at Bauer. Blackout.

SEVENTEEN

The Teacher comes into the bar and joins Julius Caesar at his table.

Teacher Hail Caesar!

Caesar It's you. The hero!

Teacher What do you mean?

Caesar You didn't have to tell them about that box. I'd never have done that. Respect!

He operates the device in his pocket that makes the eye in the skull on his tiepin light up red.

Teacher Not everyone thinks that way. I had a letter from my parents. My mother said: 'We've been awake all night.' My father said: 'What have we done to deserve this?'

Caesar Ah, well, in that case you'll be needing a drink.

Teacher Do you remember a boy called Trauner?

Caesar I certainly do. Horrible little shit.

Teacher He's the one with the fish eyes.

Caesar Of course! Of course he is. So the girl didn't do it after all!

Teacher I think I might be a bit in love with her.

Caesar Don't worry. We'll get him. I shall mobilise my troops.

Teacher It's not going to be easy. We produced witnesses to say the compass found by the body was his, but they refused to believe us. And the girl is ill. She was taken to the prison hospital with stomach cramps.

Caesar You want us to spring her? No, first things first. We'll have a few drinks. Then we'll work out how to crack that little bastard, Trauner. It's not going to be easy, as you say. His parents are extremely rich and influential, lot of Party connections. But we shall prevail. Won't we?

He operates the skull's eye again, by way of answering his question.

Teacher You were so right. The age of the fish.

Blackout.

EIGHTEEN

The Teacher's room. The Teacher is at the door, letting in the Priest, who's wearing a suit and tie.

Teacher Come in.

Priest I've been thinking about you a great deal.

Teacher Is your punishment posting over?

Priest Yes: I hardly ever wear vestments when I'm in town. But let's talk about you. I was so impressed with your testimony. You're looking good. You look as if a weight's been taken off your shoulders. You look positively cheerful.

Teacher Cheerful!

Priest Last time we met you told me you didn't believe in God.

Teacher I remember.

Priest I came to see you for a particular reason. I'm sure you're aware that, after what you said in court, you're not going to be allowed to teach anywhere in the high school system.

Teacher Yes, I knew that before I decided to make my statement.

Priest Well, I wanted to know how you intend to make a living. Judging by what you were saying about the rich, I take it you won't be living on your investments.

Teacher You're right. I have nothing. And I have my parents to support.

The Priest looks at him solemnly for a moment.

Priest I think I may be in a position to help.

Teacher In what way?

Priest I might have a job to offer.

Teacher A job?

Priest The only thing is, it would be abroad.

Teacher Where?

Priest Africa.

Teacher Africa?

Priest What's wrong with that? Africans are human beings as well.

He's puzzled by the Teacher's reaction: the Teacher considers explaining, but then simply shakes his head and smiles.

Teacher They certainly are.

Priest You'd be teaching in a mission school.

Teacher Would I have to . . . be ordained?

Priest No, not at all.

The Teacher hesitates.

Teacher I don't know.

Priest What's the difficulty?

Teacher It seems to me we white people have brought the Africans nothing but trouble. All those dirty business dealings.

Priest It's entirely up to you whether or not you choose to get involved in dirty business dealings. Your vocation is your responsibility.

Teacher Vocation?

Priest Everyone has their vocation.

Silence. The Teacher considers.

Teacher Well, thank you. I would like to accept your offer. But first I have to make sure that the girl who's been put on trial is acquitted. I happen to know the identity of the real murderer: one of the boys I teach.

Priest Have you spoken to his mother?

The Teacher is surprised by the question.

Teacher His mother?

Priest You have to tell his mother. She'll know what to do. You have to go and see her before anything else . . .

Blackout.

NINETEEN

Salon in the Trauner house. A lavishly decorated pink and gold room with eighteenth-century furniture and mythological prints. The Teacher is shown in by the Trauners' Butler.

Butler I can't guarantee Frau Trauner will be available to see you, sir.

Teacher It's an extremely important matter.

Butler Might you be able to come back tomorrow?

Teacher I told you, this concerns her son.

The Butler makes a minuscule dismissive gesture.

Butler Frau Trauner is often too busy to see her son. Even he would usually have to be announced.

Teacher Well, announce me, will you? Now.

Butler Just as you like, sir. We'll do our best. Wait here, if you'd be so kind.

He exits. The Teacher turns to the audience.

Teacher This was the grandest private house I'd ever set foot in, a huge villa in a millionaires' row out beyond the tram terminus. On the stairs on the way in, we passed an extremely famous film actress, personal friend of the Great Arsehole, well-known for her portrayal of working-class waifs. I hardly dared sit in one of those chairs, that looked as if they were waiting for Marie Antoinette to arrive for tea.

The Teacher moves over to look out of the window; a moment later, he's surprised by the arrival of Dieter Trauner.

Ah, it's you.

Trauner My mother sends her apologies. She's afraid she can't get away.

Teacher Oh? And when will she be able to get away?

Trauner I've no idea. She never has any free time.

Teacher In that case, perhaps I could have a word with your father?

Trauner He's not here. I hardly ever see him. He's always away on business.

Teacher Doesn't run a sawmill, by any chance, does he?

Trauner Not as far as I know.

Silence.

Why exactly did you want to see my parents, sir?

Pause. Trauner waits, a sudden flicker of fear in his eyes.

Teacher I wanted to have a word with them about you.

Trauner About me?

He grins, his eyes glassy.

Teacher Shame they don't have any time.

He turns to leave. Blackout.

TWENTY

The bar. Julius Caesar sits at a table with two young girls: Nelly, whom we've met before; and Lola, another blonde, a colleague of hers. The Teacher steps into the bar and joins them, noticing immediately the air of dejection at the table.

Teacher I got your note.

Caesar nods morosely and pours the Teacher a glass of schnapps from an almost-empty bottle. The Teacher nods to Nelly.

We've met before.

Nelly Oh, yeah?

Teacher Is something the matter?

Caesar We're very disappointed.

Teacher Why?

Caesar I really wanted to surprise you. The hook was baited, the fish was circling, everything was planned. Then, what do you know, he didn't bite.

Teacher You're talking about . . .?

Caesar I told you I would mobilise my troops. Get your girl out of chokey.

Teacher What happened?

Caesar Well, I arranged a rendezvous between the fish and Nelly here . . .

Teacher So it was you.

Nelly What d'you mean?

Teacher Some friends of mine have been keeping an eye on Trauner. Yesterday they told me he'd met up with a blonde lady . . .

Caesar That's right. I got Nelly to pick him up at the cinema. Then . . . well, you tell him, Nelly.

Nelly I brought him back here and took him upstairs . . .

Teacher And?

Nelly It was disgusting. Little creep! I couldn't stand him.

Teacher Why?

Nelly I don't want to talk about it. For one thing, he kept laughing while he was doing it.

Teacher Laughing?

Nelly I got so pissed off with him, I hit him. He just climbed straight off me and went and looked at his face in the mirror. He's sick.

Caesar Even so, Nelly is so heroic, she agreed to meet him again today.

Nelly Wouldn't do it for no one else.

Julius Caesar grins and illuminates the skull in his tiepin.

Lola Nelly waited two hours outside the cinema.

Nelly He stood me up.

Caesar See, we sent him a letter from Nelly saying she was in love with him and wanted to see him again tonight.

Nelly Mind you, I'm relieved the little bastard didn't show up.

Teacher What was your plan?

Caesar The idea was to reconstruct the crime.

Teacher How?

Caesar To get the fish to think he'd done it again. This time in bed.

Teacher Go on.

Caesar Nelly was going to bring him back here and get him paralytic. Then she and Lola were going to take him upstairs, let him do whatever he could manage and wait till he fell asleep. Then Nelly was going to lie on the floor under a sheet, splash a few bloodstains around. Then Lola was going to scream the place down and I was going to burst in and pretend to be the police. I was going to tell him I'd nabbed him red-handed for murder, clip him round the ear a few times and make him confess he was the one who killed Neumann. We had the whole scene worked out. I'd definitely have landed him.

Silence. The Teacher shakes his head, smiling.

Teacher But he didn't show.

Caesar That's right.

Silence. All four drink for a while, pensive. Caesar shakes his head.

It isn't only your girl I'm thinking about. What about that poor boy he killed?

Teacher I'm afraid he was a ghastly little prick.

Caesar Quite possibly. Very likely. All the same . . .

Another melancholy pause. Blackout.

TWENTY-ONE

The Teacher's room. Night. The Teacher stands looking out of the window. Suddenly, he senses something and turns round abruptly. Standing in the room, dressed in his Pioneer's uniform, is Otto Neumann.

Neumann You're partly responsible for my murder, aren't you, sir?

Teacher No, I . . .

Neumann You were the one broke into the box.

Teacher Yes, but . . .

Neumann I said to you: 'Please help me, sir!' And you said you would. But you didn't. I know you think it's all in the past . . .

He breaks off. Silence. The Teacher shakes his head, trying perhaps to dispel the vision.

Last winter, sir, you gave us a history lesson, do you remember? You said that in the Middle Ages, before an execution, the hangman always asked the murderer for forgiveness for the great wrong he was about to do him. You said guilt could only be redeemed by guilt.

The Teacher starts to move swiftly towards the door, but Neumann blocks his way.

Stop! Why do you only think about yourself?

Teacher Do I?

Neumann All you're thinking about is the fish. But you're the fish.

Teacher How do you make that out?

Neumann I just explained to you: the hangman and the murderer; at a certain point, they blend into one another. And you're already starting to feel sorry for him.

Teacher I don't think . . .

Neumann You don't think about me. The only reason you want to catch the fish is because of that girl. Why is that?

Teacher The way she looked at me in the courtroom. With those big, sad eyes.

Neumann She doesn't have big eyes. She has shifty little close-together eyes. The eyes of a thief.

Teacher A thief?

Neumann The eyes you saw in the courtroom weren't her eyes. They were someone else's.

Teacher Whose?

Neumann vanishes, leaving the Teacher troubled and disoriented. A sudden loud bang on the door almost makes him jump out of his skin.

Who is it?

Voice (*offstage*) Police.

The Teacher, afraid now, cautiously opens the door. A uniformed Policeman stands in the doorway.

Teacher What do you want?

Policeman There's a car downstairs, sir, we'd like you to come with us.

Teacher What for?

Policeman Just some information, sir. It'll all be explained.

Blackout.

TWENTY-TWO

The Policeman leads the Teacher into the salon in the Trauner house. There are a number of people already in the room: a couple more policemen, an Inspector sitting at a desk, the Butler and Frau Trauner, a glamorous woman in a low-cut, backless evening gown. The Policeman leads the Teacher over to the Inspector, who looks up at him for a moment.

Inspector I understand you came to visit this lady yesterday afternoon?

The Teacher looks across at Frau Trauner. She's glaring back at him, hatred in her eyes.

Answer the question, please.

Teacher Oh, yes. I came to visit her, but she didn't have time to see me.

Inspector And what did you want to speak to her about?

Teacher Her son. I wanted to tell her I had certain suspicions regarding her son.

Frau Trauner leaps to her feet.

Frau Trauner He's a liar! It's all lies! It's all his fault, everything! He drove my son to his death!

Teacher What?

Inspector Silence!

He hands the Teacher a scrap of paper.

This was found next to his body.

The Teacher reads aloud from the scrap of paper.

Teacher 'The teacher has driven me to this . . .'

He looks up, and across at Frau Trauner.

Is this all there was? It looks as if it's been torn in half.

Frau Trauner looks away.

Inspector That's all there was. Would you be kind enough to explain it to us?

Teacher I'd become convinced it was this boy who murdered Otto Neumann.

Inspector Would you tell us why?

Teacher He liked to watch. He wanted to experience birth and death and everything that came in between. He wanted to know every secret, not out of love of knowledge, but so that he could feel superior to it. His love of reality was really only hatred of the truth. He wasn't anything like those children in the village in the mountains who sit in the windows painting dolls.

Inspector What does that have to do with anything?

Frau Trauner has turned back to look at the Teacher. She's staring at him now, wild-eyed. He returns her gaze.

Teacher Yes, it's quite possible I drove your son to death.

Frau Trauner suddenly becomes hysterical and launches herself at the Teacher. It's not clear if she's laughing or crying, planning to attack the Teacher or embrace him. One of the policemen intercepts her; there's a brief struggle, as a result of which a scrap of paper flutters to the ground. The Policeman picks it up and hands it to the Inspector, who reads it. Then he picks up the other scrap of paper and fits the two pieces together. He reads aloud.

Inspector 'The teacher has driven me to this, because he knows I killed Otto Neumann with a rock.'

Silence. Frau Trauner, is still now. She takes a deep breath and speaks to the Inspector.

Frau Trauner I just wanted to spare the family the shame of all this. But as soon as he started talking about those children sitting in the window, I thought: what's the point?

Blackout.

TWENTY-THREE

The Teacher's room: table in the window, map of the world on the wall. But the atmosphere has completely changed. Bright light slants in through louvres and we can hear all the rich, buzzing and humming sounds of a tropical afternoon. We are in Africa. The Teacher, in shirtsleeves, perches on a corner of his table, looking out at us.

Teacher So now I know. God is Truth.

I went to see Eva before I left and discovered that the ghost was quite right. She has the eyes of a thief. I got the priest to promise me he would look after her when she comes out of jail. Meanwhile, Ziegler, who had learned in the most shocking possible way that Eva did not love him, is free to get on with his life.

Julius Caesar gave me a present.

He lifts the skull tiepin off the table and operates its winking eye.

I left nothing behind. I brought everything with me.

Because I understood there was no going back. Not the way Europe is now, driving as fast as it can towards a brick wall.

Besides, I feel completely at home here.

Here among the Africans.